THE

Power

OF

THANKSGIVING

THE

Power

OF
THANKSGIVING

APOSTLE. DR. ROBERT H. RAGLAND

XULON PRESS

Xulon Press
2301 Lucien Way #415
Maitland, FL 32751
407.339.4217
www.xulonpress.com

Printed in the United States of America.

Paperback ISBN-13: 978-1-6628-0393-2
eBook ISBN-13: 978-1-6628-0394-9

TABLE OF CONTENTS

INTRODUCTION

IN THIS BOOK, *The Power of Thanksgiving*, you are about to discover the power behind your thanksgiving. Singing with our hands lifted up and our mouths filled with praise, with a heart of thanksgiving, I will bless Thee, O Lord. Have we ever considered the power of our thanksgiving to God? Many times, in our lives, our hearts have been overwhelmed with negative experiences; but has your heart ever been overwhelmed with the power of thanksgiving to God? God created life for believers to experience the power of thanksgiving. The clapping of hands and the stomping of the feet are acts of praise because our hearts are overwhelmed. The transformation power of praise is to present praise as the overwhelming transformative event in the lives of every believer. This is the inner authorization of what God has approved to be manifested from the unseen to the seen.

Thanksgiving is the heartbeat of every miracle and supernatural act of the Father. When God does miracles, He knows Thanksgiving will be offered; it is the inevitability of the Godward expression of God being Himself. The miracles produce the praises that go back to God. When the praise is not given, it is us rejecting the product that God has released. Thanksgiving is due to God for all the things that He has done in our life that describe that He is worthy of all the honor, praise, and glory. God knows the essence of our heartbeat and He knows what it takes to move us from the natural to the Spiritual of meeting our every need. It is our personal deliverance.

In 1990, the Lord spoke to me, saying, "The Gates of Thanksgiving surround the courts of praise; the bells of Thanksgiving do not cease to play when the demonstration of praise begins; they operate in unison." And He continued to speak to me and say, "Thanksgiving is the heart of joy."

In preparation of reading this book I encourage you to have an open heart, a comprehensive mind, and a humble spirit to receive revelatory insight.

Acknowledgement

I WOULD LIKE TO acknowledge and thank those that have helped me on this journey of completing *The Power of Thanksgiving*. Elder Dominique Bryant who initiated the writing of this book and spent countless hours with me to push it forward and make it a reality. I would also like to thank the following individuals for their assistance: Apostle Tamesha Q. Fulmore and Elder Tonya Ruffin. A special thanks to Apostles Lawrence and Omolara Olaniyi; it is because of your sacrifice and giving heart that this is possible. I will forever be thankful to you.

To my wife Ruby Ragland, thank you for thirty-nine years of standing and supporting me in ministry and marriage. I love you.

FOREWORD

UPON MEETING THIS amazing man of God, Apostle Dr. Robert H. Ragland, in 2002 at the Department of Probation as my back-up supervisor, my life has never been the same. I evolved into a Pastor and Apostle through his outstanding leadership. God has given us a Jonathan/David relationship which propelled me into my inevitable gifts and calling. Apostle Ragland, the Senior Apostle/Pastor at Victorious Triumphant Word International Church (VTWIC) is a true prophet and mouthpiece of God who immediately began to expel the unadulterated Word of God fearlessly in my life, holding nothing back, which emboldened and empowered me for ministry. He worked as the President of Victorious College of Theology (VCOT), while teaching and mentoring me as Dean. His teaching has transformed many students into leadership at VCOT.

I stand astonished at the level of wisdom Apostle Ragland has demonstrated while teaching, preaching, and pastoring. Truly he has no fears of man, but fears

God and will give you the absolute truth as God downloads it to him. Like a sponge, I sat at the feet of this awesome teacher, eagerly soaking in and applying what I have gleaned to mirror the God in him.

Just as Jesus was and is a servant, Apostle Ragland served not only his members at VTWIC but many churches, friends, families, and acquaintances untiringly nationwide. He financed innumerable books and CDs in my life and the lives of countless others as well. He has invested in the call upon my life as his **successor,** and I am ever so grateful that God raised Apostle Ragland to be my mentor, counselor, and lifetime friend.

I can guarantee that this book will change your life and propel you into the high calling of God. You will never be the same as you allow this life altering word to transform your mind. God has allowed Apostle Ragland through this book to fulfill Ephesians 4:11-13: "And He gave some Apostles, Prophets, Evangelists, Pastors and Teachers for the perfecting of the saints; for the work of the ministry; for the edifying of the body of Christ; till we all come in the unity of the faith and of the knowledge of the Son of God unto a perfect man, unto the measure of the stature of the fullness of Christ."

Apostle, Dr. Tamesha Q. Fulmore, Pastor V.T.W.I.C.

CHAPTER ONE

WHAT IS THANKSGIVING?

WHEN MOST PEOPLE hear the word thanksgiving, they tend to think of the freshly carved oven-roasted turkey, sweet potato pie, green bean casserole, and home-made cranberry sauce while others think it's just a mere expression a person gives.

Throughout this book we will have the opportunity to search through the Scriptures and learn that thanksgiving has much more substance in its definition, spiritually, than most of us have understood throughout our years.

Thanksgiving is:

1. **The Expression of Joy Godward:**
Everything that's good comes from the Lord. Thanksgiving is the celebration of God's joy and our internal reciprocation for His provision, blessings, healing, etc. Thanksgiving is a down payment of

what God has done, is doing, and will do in your life that is considered good. And by good we mean good.

2. The Characteristics of the Fruit of the Spirit:

Thanksgiving is our inner attitude towards God. Oftentimes we mistaken the act of thanksgiving as being external. We go to church and the worship leader says, "Let's give God some praise and thanks!" and we clap our hands and stomp our feet without the understanding that it all begins within. Thanksgiving is the mirror image of each fruit of the spirit recorded in Galatians 5:22-23. Without thanksgiving we can't love as God loves, we can't have joy, we can't be a carrier of peace, it's impossible to mirror forbearance, we can't show real kindness and goodness and we can't be gentle and have self-control.

3. To Acknowledge Fully:

Faith is like a stream or a river flowing but the power of the flow and its ability to accomplish its assignment is the thanksgiving that precedes. Thanksgiving is the response to God's will being manifested and without thanksgiving there is no manifestation. In other words, the greater the thanksgiving the greater the manifestation in quantity and quality.

4. The Celebration in Praise:

One of God's greatest gifts is Godly Thanksgiving. Thanksgiving from God and giving to God has no boundaries. Most of our apartments and homes are 110 volt and an adapter is necessary to connect it to an electrical apparatus, and so it is with thanksgiving. It connects us to every other aspect to the will of God, the plan of God, and the activity of God. When we come in alignment with true thanksgiving the only thing left to do is to open our mouths and give God a praise.

5. The Expression of Gratitude:

God always makes the life of a believer better and brighter through showers of blessings. There are many examples of thanksgiving in our everyday lives. Faith may produce the car but thanksgiving is the fuel that propels the vehicle forward. Your gratefulness and gratitude allow God to give you the various levels of success in your life.

Chapter Two

What Does the Word Say about Thanksgiving?

THE CHARACTERISTICS OF thanksgiving can be found in multiple texts throughout the Bible. In this chapter we will take the time to unfold the biblical references leading us to Bible-based clarity on the power of thanksgiving.

1. **Thanksgiving is spiritual sacrifice:**
   The sacrifice of thanksgiving is composed of various ingredients: the lifting of our hands, the opening of our mouths, and, most importantly, the heart of gratitude. This can be done on our knees, standing, or even lying in your bed; there is no position your body must be in. However, our heart must be positioned on and in God. Thanksgiving is directed to God Himself, and we

must always remember that thanksgiving always comes from the heart.

Psalms 116:17 King James Version (KJV)
I will offer to thee the sacrifice of thanksgiving and will call upon the name of the LORD.

Psalm 116:17 Amplified Bible (AMP)
I will offer to You the sacrifice of thanksgiving,
And will call on the name of the LORD.

Psalm 116:17-19 The Message (MSG)
What can I give back to GOD
for the blessings he's poured out on me?
I'll lift high the cup of salvation—a toast to GOD!
I'll pray in the name of GOD;
I'll complete what I promised GOD I'd do,
and I'll do it together with his people.
When they arrive at the gates of death,
GOD welcomes those who love him.
Oh, GOD, here I am, your servant,
your faithful servant: set me free for your service!
I'm ready to offer the thanksgiving sacrifice
and pray in the name of GOD.

I'll complete what I promised GOD I'd do,
and I'll do it in company with his people,
In the place of worship, in GOD's house,
in Jerusalem, GOD's city.
Hallelujah!

2. Thanksgiving is a Duty:

Thanksgiving is an exclusive entity reserved for God Himself. As blood-washed believers we are duty bound to offer our thanksgiving to the God Himself who has assigned thanksgiving to Himself. Isn't that something to think about? Thanksgiving actually belongs to God! It is our duty to give Him what belongs to Him. Our thanksgiving is far from natural. Although we may use our mouths to give thanks, we cannot give thanks without words; but those words that we give should proceed from the Spirit of God.

The Spirit of God gives life, and God's Word is life. When we give thanksgiving, we are giving light and life to every area of our life. Where there is life there is deliverance. God wants all of His children free. It's in freedom where we grow, live, and dwell in liberty.

When you are free you cannot help yourself but to give thanksgiving to the One by whom it is deserved.

Thanksgiving is the fullness of what God wants. Not only does God want thanksgiving but He freely wants to give it to you. What greater freedom than what Christ gives us?

2 Thessalonians 2:13 King James Version (KJV)

13 But we are bound to give thanks always to God for you, brethren beloved of the Lord, because God hath from the beginning chosen you to salvation through sanctification of the Spirit and belief of the truth:

2 Thessalonians 2:13 Amplified Bible (AMP)

13 But we should and are [morally] obligated [as debtors] always to give thanks to God for you, believers beloved by the Lord, because God has chosen you from the beginning for salvation through the [a]sanctifying work of the Spirit [that sets you apart for God's purpose] and by your faith in the truth [of God's word that leads you to spiritual maturity].

2 Thessalonians 2:13-14 The Message (MSG)

13-14 Meanwhile, we've got our hands full continually thanking God for you, our good friends—so loved by God! God picked you out as his from the very start. Think of it: included in God's original plan of salvation by the bond of faith in the living truth. This is the life of the Spirit he invited you to through the Message we delivered, in which you get in on the glory of our Master, Jesus Christ.

3. Thanksgiving is Unleashing:

You cannot catch something that has not yet been released, so it is imperative that we release our thanksgiving so that we are in the position to catch what God has ordained for us to catch.

Thanksgiving makes something unavailable now available. This is the reason why it's so powerful. When you look at the supernatural, it has to have room made for it. It's not a natural occurrence, so our flesh tends to shy away from it because it is of the unfamiliar. However, in the spirit, it is as natural as natural can be. Your spirit delights in the manifestation of anything that glorifies God.

It's the same with Thanksgiving. Once you realize that thanksgiving is spiritual it will begin to open divine avenues in your life that only thanksgiving can unlock. We need not to ever underestimate or undervalue the power of thanksgiving. Thanksgiving can call forth things that be not, according to the Word, as though they already were. I may not have joy, but my thanksgiving allows me to enter in into it.

Thanksgiving is your spirit communicating with the Spirit of God and His Spirit communicating with your spirit. Therefore, all thanksgiving to God is an impartation of the Spirit of God.

Ephesians 1:16 King James Version (KJV)
16 Cease not to give thanks for you, making mention of you in my prayers.

Ephesians 1:16 Amplified Version
16 I do not cease to give thanks for you, remembering you in my prayers;

Ephesians 1:15-19 Message Bible

15-19 That's why, when I heard of the solid trust you have in the Master Jesus and your outpouring of love to all the followers of Jesus, I couldn't stop thanking God for you—every time I prayed, I'd think of you and give thanks. But I do more than thank. I ask—ask the

4. Thanksgiving is Spontaneous

True thanksgiving is not a religious act, but it is a heart response to who God is to you personally. The power of thanksgiving can be used at any time and in any and every situation. Thanksgiving has no borders. Its ability to break through walls, barriers, chains, and shackles is limitless through the power of God.

If you ever find yourself in a place where you are bound, whether it be little or small, the power of your thanksgiving in the midst of your fetter will meet you right where you are the moment you open up your mouth to declare your thanksgiving. Rejoicing is your personal declaration that even though you may appear bound, your reality is that you are free the moment you give God praise.

Philippians 1:13 King James Version (KJV)
So that my bonds in Christ are manifest in all the palace, and in all other places;

Philippians 1:13 Amplified Bible (AMP)
My imprisonment in [the cause of] Christ has become common knowledge throughout the whole [a]praetorian (imperial) guard and to everyone else.

Philippians 1:13-14 The Message (MSG)
[12-14] I want to report to you, friends, that my imprisonment here has had the opposite of its intended effect. Instead of being squelched, the Message has actually prospered. All the soldiers here, and everyone else, too, found out that I'm in jail because of this Messiah. That piqued their curiosity, and now they've learned all about him. Not only that, but most of the followers of Jesus here have become far more sure of themselves in the faith than ever, speaking out fearlessly about God, about the Messiah.

5. Thanksgiving offered in Christs' Name

As born-again believers we have the privilege to be seated in Christ Jesus, who sits with His Father in heavenly places and in victory. In this position we have no choice but to give Christ all the glory, majesty, praise, and honor because it rightfully belongs to Him. Victory is a position of greatness.

Ephesians 5:20 King James Version

Giving thanks always for all things unto God and the Father in the name of our Lord Jesus Christ

Ephesians 5:20 Amplified Bible

Always giving thanks to God the Father for all things, in the name of our Lord Jesus Christ

Ephesians 5:20 The Message Bible

Do not drink too much wine. That cheapens your life. Drink the Spirit of God, huge draughts of him. Sing hymns instead of drinking songs! Sing songs from your heart to Christ. Sing praises over everything, any excuse for a song to God the Father in the name of our Master, Jesus Christ.

6. **Thanksgiving offered in every circumstance of life**

   The word of God in its infallible nature instructs us to give thanks in all things. What does that mean? Does this mean that in your worst moments and toughest situations that thanksgiving is required? There is only one clear and precise answer and that would be: absolutely, yes! No matter the situation, thanksgiving is always required.

According to God's Word, thanksgiving is the will of God. It is also God's will for the attributes of thanksgiving to be operative in every situation and every circumstance, day, or night, in your life. It's easy to give God thanks in your great moments when life is going well and it seems that every mountain in your life has been made into plains and every storm has seemed to cease. But can you thank Him when all is going wrong? When the mountains are too high to climb and you cannot seem to see your way through the storm?

When thanksgiving becomes a part of your life, it allows those negative circumstances to hear your faith through your praise. You stand on every promise that has been made to you through His Word. Thanksgiving builds your faith, gives you strength, and reminds you that there is no mountain, storm, or circumstance that is greater than your God.

1 Thessalonians 5:18 King James Version

18 In every thing give thanks: for this is the will of God in Christ Jesus concerning you.

1 Thessalonians 5:18 Amplified Bible

18 in every situation [no matter what the circumstances] be thankful and continually give thanks to God; for this is the will of God for you in Christ Jesus.

1 Thessalonians 5:16-18 The Message Bible

16-18 Be cheerful no matter what; pray all the time; thank God no matter what happens. This is the way God wants you who belong to Christ Jesus to live.

8. Thanksgiving offered in all prayers

Thanksgiving is always a sign of victory. Therefore, everything I say and do in the name of Jesus Christ is always victorious. When we pray our focus should always be to pray the victory and not the problem. If you don't have food in your home how would you pray?

1. Father, in the name of Jesus, I do not have milk, I do not have meat; Lord, I do not have bread.

2. Father, in the name of Jesus, Your Word promised me according to Philippians 4:19 that You would supply all my needs according to Your riches and glory in Christ Jesus. You also promised me in Psalms 37: 25 that you have never seen the righteous forsaken nor his seed begging bread. So, Father I thank You for my miracle now in the name of Jesus.

Although both prayers were from the heart and it addressed the same problem, one was praying the problem and the other was thanking God for the victory.

Philippians 4:6 King James Version
⁶ Be careful for nothing; but in everything by prayer and supplication with thanksgiving let your requests be made known unto God.

Philippians 4:6 Amplified Bible
⁶ Do not be anxious or worried about anything, but in everything [every circumstance and situation] by prayer and petition with thanksgiving, continue to make your [specific] requests known to God.

Philippians 4:6-7 The Message

6-7 Don't fret or worry. Instead of worrying, pray. Let petitions and praises shape your worries into prayers, letting God know your concerns. Before you know it, a sense of God's wholeness, everything coming together for good, will come and settle you down. It's wonderful what happens when Christ displaces worry at the center of your life.

9. Thanksgiving gives courage:

In this Christian walk we are guaranteed to go through troubles. Although hard times and storms are sure to come, we are also guaranteed victory over every obstacle. Our Thanksgiving is a symbol of our victory. Praise during a storm reminds us that victory is already ours. The manifestation of victory lets you know that you are an overcomer and that there is nothing, absolutely nothing too hard for our God. No storm, no mountain, and no situation can stand up to the victory attached to your praise. So, when you go through your next storm remember there is a bonfire of victory waiting at the end of your praise.

Acts 28:1 King James Version

28 And when they were escaped, then they knew that the island was called Melita.

Acts 28:1 Amplified Bible

28 After we were safe [on land], we found out that the island was called [a]Malta.

Acts 28:1-2 The Message Bible

28 [1-2] Once everyone was accounted for and we realized we had all made it, we learned that we were on the island of Malta. The natives went out of their way to be friendly to us. The day was rainy and cold and we were already soaked to the bone, but they built a huge bonfire and gathered us around it.

Chapter Three

Characteristics of Nurturing Your Faith

THANKSGIVING ENLARGES THE borders of your faith. It has the ability to reach beyond where your faith is currently and escort you to where your faith needs to be to experience your victory. If you need healing, give God thanksgiving for it now. If you need deliverance, thank Him for it now. If you need breakthrough, thank Him for it now. Your thanksgiving is assigned to your manifestation. You will recognize the depth of your faith when you reach the height of your thanksgiving.

2 Thessalonians 1:3 King James Version
We are bound to thank God always for you, brethren, as it is meet, because that your faith groweth exceedingly, and the charity of every one of you all toward each other aboundeth;

2 Thessalonians 1:3 Amplified Bible

We ought always *and* indeed are morally obligated [as those in debt] to give thanks to God for you, [a] brothers and sisters, as is fitting, because your faith is growing ever greater, and the [unselfish] [b]love of each one of you toward one another is continually increasing.

2 Thessalonians 1:3 The Message Bible

You need to know, friends, that thanking God over and over for you is not only a pleasure; it's a must. We *have* to do it. Your faith is growing phenomenally; your love for each other is developing wonderfully. Why, it's only right that we give thanks. We're so proud of you; you're so steady and determined in your faith despite all the hard times that have come down on you. We tell everyone we meet in the churches all about you.

A. Produces the attitude of submission

The highest form of thanksgiving to be thankful for salvation. When your heart is overwhelmed with the truth of who Christ is to you as a born-again believer, you now have the power to walk in the newness of who Christ has made you to be. How powerful is that? I can now submit my old person to Christ so that I can now be adorned with my new person.

Ephesians 4:20-22 King James Version

But ye have not so learned Christ; If so be that ye have heard him, and have been taught by him, as the truth is in Jesus: That ye put off concerning the former conversation the old man, which is corrupt according to the deceitful lusts;

Ephesians 4:20-22 Amplified Bible

But you did not learn Christ in this way! If in fact you have [really] heard Him and have been taught by Him, just as truth is in Jesus [revealed in His life and personified in Him], that, regarding your previous way of life, you put off your old self [completely discard your former nature], which is being corrupted through deceitful desires,

Ephesians 4:20-22 The Message Bible

But that's no life for you. You learned Christ! My assumption is that you have paid careful attention to him, been well instructed in the truth precisely as we have it in Jesus. Since, then, we do not have the excuse of ignorance, everything—and I do mean everything—connected with that old way of life has to go. It's rotten through and through. Get rid of it! And then take on an entirely new way of life—a God-fashioned life, a life renewed from the inside and working itself into your conduct as God accurately reproduces his character in you.

CHAPTER FOUR

THE OPPOSITE OF THANKSGIVING

IN THE PREVIOUS chapters we have had the opportunity to search the Scriptures and define and comprehend thanksgiving in ways that most have never looked at Thanksgiving before. Before diving into our next topic, please take the time to read and study Deuteronomy 28:45-48. The three versions are given to you to help to illuminate your understanding and give you an opportunity to take apart and digest what the Word of God is showing us through the revelation of Scripture.

Deuteronomy 28:45-48 (KJV)
Moreover all these curses shall come upon thee, and shall pursue thee, and overtake thee, till thou be destroyed; because thou hearkenedst not unto the voice of the LORD thy God, to keep his commandments and his statutes which he commanded

thee: And they shall be upon thee for a sign and for a wonder, and upon thy seed forever. Because thou servedst not the LORD thy God with joyfulness, and with gladness of heart, for the abundance of all things; Therefore shalt thou serve thine enemies which the LORD shall send against thee, in hunger, and in thirst, and in nakedness, and in want of all things: and he shall put a yoke of iron upon thy neck, until he have destroyed thee.

Signs Opposite of Thanksgiving
1. Ingratitude
2. Complaining
3. Every form and representative of self-pity
4. Being unappreciative

The signs listed above are the fruits of an ungrateful heart. To be ungrateful is an attitude. It's a set way of thinking not only in your mind but also deep down in the corridors of your heart. I can boldly say that when we have an ungrateful attitude we are nowhere close to pleasing God. Isn't that what this walk is all about? Wanting to please the Creator not only in His image but also in His likeness. Could you imagine giving someone your most precious and valuable goods and they do not have the heart to say thank you? Our Father gave us His only begotten son and all that is good and perfect is in Him. Isn't that something! Therefore the Word of God tells us in 1 Thessalonians 5:18, "In everything give thanks: for this is the will of God in Christ Jesus concerning you."

Does that mean in the bad times? Absolutely!

Does that mean in the turbulent times? Absolutely!

Does that mean in the midst of the storm? Absolutely!

It is crucial for us to hold on to a heart, mind, and spirit of thanksgiving always. The essence of ungratefulness is murmuring. Murmuring comes from an unthankful heart caused by the absence of the strength of God to control your tongue and its confessions.

To eliminate this obstacle, God said in Philippians 2:13-14, "For it is God which worketh in you to will and to do of His good pleasure. Do all things without murmuring and disputing."

Thanksgiving of the heart leads to the joy of the Lord, and the joy of the Lord strengthens the inner man which gives us the peace of God daily. This is why we can give thanks in the midst of every obstacle.

CHAPTER FIVE

BENEFITS OF THE POWER OF THANKSGIVING

AS WE CONCLUDE this study, we dare not leave out the benefits of the power of thanksgiving. There are ten benefits along with corresponding Scriptures and nuggets that you will want to hold dear to your heart. This study was developed to not only define Thanksgiving and its power but also to reveal the victory that belongs to you when you live a thankful life. It is my hope and prayer that from this day forward thanksgiving will be an attitude you attribute, and your praise and worship will never be the same.

1. **Thanksgiving is the power of focus:**
   One of the main assignments of the devil is to knock you off course and to derail you from God's perfect will. Satan wants to blur or double your vision so that you are unable to count your blessings and to keep

you out of the will of God. So, when you feel like your focus is off remember to tap into your thanksgiving. Make a list of His goodness, whether it is a mental list or a list with pen and paper. Meditate on those things and remember that focus is one of your greatest weapons.

James 1:8 King James Version (KJV)

2. **Thanksgiving is the choice to focus on the Giver rather than the need:**
   Thanksgiving is a deliberate act to focus on God. Choice is a powerful thing. When you use the power of choice to focus on the One to whom Thanksgiving belongs you have accessed the key to remain victorious in every situation of life.

Philippians 4:8 King James Version (KJV)
Finally, brethren, whatsoever things are true, whatsoever things are honest, whatsoever things are just, whatsoever things are pure, whatsoever things are lovely, whatsoever things are of good report; if there be any virtue, and if there be any praise, think on these things.

3. Thanksgiving is the turning point to God:

Thanksgiving always moves us toward God, and it is reserved for the One who creates every reason to give thanks.

4. Thanksgiving is the power of God opening the gates:

Thanksgiving is the key to open doors. How many doors have remained closed in our lives because we did not approach with our key of thanksgiving? This gives us all a lot to think about. What will be your approach to the next closed door in your life? Give thanks.

Psalms 100:4 King James Version (KJV)

⁴Enter into his gates with thanksgiving, and into his courts with praise: be thankful unto him, and bless his name.

5. Thanksgiving releases the supernatural power of God:

You cannot live a supernatural life without living a thankful life. One of the greatest examples are found right here in:

John 6:10-13 King James Version (KJV)

And Jesus said, Make the men sit down. Now there was much grass in the place. So, the men sat down, in number about five thousand. And Jesus took the loaves; and when he had given thanks, he distributed to the disciples, and the disciples to them that were set down; and likewise of the fishes as much as they would. When they were filled, he said unto his disciples, Gather up the fragments that remain, that nothing be lost. Therefore they gathered them together, and filled twelve baskets with the fragments of the five barley loaves, which remained over and above unto them that had eaten.

Jesus raised Lazarus from the dead.

John 11:4 King James Version (KJV)

When Jesus heard that, he said, This sickness is not unto death, but for the glory of God, that the Son of God might be glorified thereby.

6. **Thanksgiving release the power of peace:**
   Peace can often be misunderstood. How can you have peace in the midst of chaos or when your back is

pinned up against the wall and you have nowhere to turn? Through your thanksgiving, God will give you a peace that can't be explained by words or understood by the human mind. It's a supernatural peace only given by God.

Philippians 4:6-8 King James Version (KJV)

Be careful for nothing; but in everything by prayer and supplication with thanksgiving let your requests be made known unto God. And the peace of God, which passeth all understanding, shall keep your hearts and minds through Christ Jesus. Finally, brethren, whatsoever things are true, whatsoever things are honest, whatsoever things are just, whatsoever things are pure, whatsoever things are lovely, whatsoever things are of good report; if there be any virtue, and if there be any praise, think on these things.

7. Thanksgiving is offered on the altar of righteous living:

Living a thankful life in Christ requires you to stand in righteousness before our Father. When you are in good standing with the Father, you have unlimited access to everything He gives you freely.

Psalms 26:4-7

[4] I have not sat with vain persons, neither will I go in with dissemblers. I have hated the congregation of evil doers; and will not sit with the wicked. I will wash mine hands in innocence: so, will I compass thine altar, O LORD: That I may publish with the voice of thanksgiving, and tell of all thy wondrous works.

8. **Thanksgiving is evidence of preparation in antic-ipation/expectancy of entering into the pres-ence of God:**

Through your praise and thanksgiving, we can see your anticipation and faith in what God can do for you, with you, and through you. It demonstrates your readiness and expectation of God's promises while standing firmly upon your unshakeable faith for its manifestation.

Psalms 95:2 King James Version (KJV)

Let us come before his presence with thanksgiving, and make a joyful noise unto him with psalms.

9. Thanksgiving precedes praise:

Thanksgiving is the first step to praise. Without thanksgiving there is no praise.

Psalms 100

Make a joyful noise unto the LORD, all ye lands. Serve the LORD with gladness: come before his presence with singing. Know ye that the LORD he is God: it is he that hath made us, and not we ourselves; we are his people, and the sheep of his pasture. Enter into his gates with thanksgiving, and into his courts with praise: be thankful unto him, and bless his name. For the LORD is good; his mercy is everlasting; and his truth endureth to all generations.

10. Thanksgiving declares that God has given me the victory:

When you get to a place in life where you can give God thanks in every situation, that is when you know that you walk and live in victory.

1 Corinthians 14:15-17

[15] What is it then? I will pray with the spirit, and I will pray with the understanding also: I will sing

with the spirit, and I will sing with the understanding also. Else when thou shalt bless with the spirit, how shall he that occupieth the room of the unlearned say Amen at thy giving of thanks, seeing he understandeth not what thou sayest? For thou verily givest thanks well, but the other is not edified.

Chapter Six

My Testimony

I HAVE BEEN A born-again believer since the age of fifteen. I was introduced to Christ by a local pastor who was a community-led leader. He reached out to those who many thoughts were unreachable. I was a resident of the New York City projects at that time, predominately a minority community. Early in my church experience I always believed that I was called to a pastoral ministry. Throughout my educational years that call only intensified. It was at Lincoln University (PA) that I accepted the call of being a pastor. During my tenure at Lincoln I experienced the power of God that transformed my life forever and spiritually awakened the gifts of the Spirit. From that time, I was so enthralled with God that the power of thanksgiving was upon me, and because of that thanksgiving I experienced the miraculous power of God.

The miraculous power of God healed me twice, from cancer and a heart attack. I believe that it was the power of thanksgiving that preserved my life, released the power of healing to supernaturally heal my body of cancer, and allowed my heart to fully recover.

The ultimate outcome of living a life with the power of thanksgiving is that I entered pastoral ministry, initiated a ministry, started a Bible school, trained elders, and Apostles, and mentored many leaders. I have participated in worldwide evangelistic ministry in the continent of Africa.

As you have read my testimony, it is my prayer that God will use you in His own way or in similar ways, in Jesus Christ's almighty name. I hope you will experience the power of thanksgiving in God.

Chapter Seven

Scriptures in Support of Giving God Thanksgiving

OUR JOURNEY IN the power of thanksgiving has come to an end, but we will continue to walk in Christ to see and experience what the power of thanksgiving can and will do in our lives. It is my personal belief that the giving of thanksgiving is one of the greatest gifts that God has given us to live a victorious life.

The Word of God provides a substance and an essence of our praise and worship, and it is a continual guide to releasing thanksgiving to the King of Kings and the Lord of Lords. The preceding Scriptures from the Word of God are meant to encourage and strengthen your walk with Father God to live an empowered life of thanksgiving.

Prayerfully, the following Scriptures will flood your life with the power of thanksgiving, and you will forever be transformed and renewed. These are some of the Scriptures about thanksgiving, as we are all called to minister to Him with hymns and spiritual melody in our hearts (Ephesians 5:19).

Psalm 7:17—I will give thanks to the LORD because of his righteousness; I will sing the praises of the name of the LORD Most High.

Psalm 9:1—I will give thanks to you, Lord, with all my heart; I will tell of all your wonderful deeds.

Psalm 34:1-3—I will extol the Lord at all times; His praise will always be on my lips. I will glory in the Lord; let the afflicted hear and rejoice. Glorify the Lord with me; let us exalt His name together

Psalm 44:4-8—You are my King and my God, who decrees victories for Jacob. Through you we push back our enemies; through your name we trample our foes. I put no trust in my bow, my sword does not bring me victory; but you give us victory over our enemies, you put our adversaries to shame. In God we make our boast all day long, and we will praise your name forever.

Psalm 50:14-15—Sacrifice thank offerings to God, fulfill your vows to the Most High, and call on me in the day of trouble; I will deliver you, and you will honor me.

Psalm 69:29—But as for me, afflicted and in pain may your salvation, God, protect me

Psalm 100:1-5—Shout for joy to the Lord, all the earth. Worship the Lord with gladness; come before him with joyful songs. Know that the Lord is God. It is He who made us, and we are his; we are His people, the sheep of His pasture. Enter His gates with Thanksgiving and his courts with praise; give thanks to Him and praise His name. For the Lord is good and His love endures forever; His faithfulness continues through all generations.

Psalm 105:1-3—Give praise to the Lord, proclaim His name, make known among the nations what He has done. Sing to Him, sing praise to Him, tell of all His wonderful acts. Glory in His holy name; let the hearts of those who seek the Lord rejoice.

n can be obtained
ing.com
USA
42240221
V00005B/1552

Psalm 106:1-3—Praise the Lord. Give th Lord, fore He is good; His love endures ' can proclaim the mighty acts of th declare His praise?

Psalm 107:1-3—Give thanks t good; His love endures forev the Lord tell their story th hand of the foe, those F from east and west, frc